Big Cats

Cougars

by Marie Brandle

Bullfrog Books

Ideas for Parents and Teachers

Bullfrog Books let children practice reading informational text at the earliest reading levels. Repetition, familiar words, and photo labels support early readers.

Before Reading

- Discuss the cover photo. What does it tell them?
- Look at the picture glossary together. Read and discuss the words.

Read the Book

- "Walk" through the book and look at the photos. Let the child ask questions. Point out the photo labels.
- Read the book to the child, or have him or her read independently.

After Reading

- Prompt the child to think more. Ask: What did you know about cougars before reading this book? What more would you like to learn about them?

Bullfrog Books are published by Jump!
5357 Penn Avenue South
Minneapolis, MN 55419
www.jumplibrary.com

Library of Congress Cataloging-in-Publication Data

Names: Brandle, Marie, 1989– author.
Title: Cougars / by Marie Brandle.
Description: Minneapolis, MN: Jump!, Inc., [2021]
Series: Big cats | Includes index.
Audience: Ages 5–8 | Audience: Grades K–1
Identifiers: LCCN 2020022617 (print)
LCCN 2020022618 (ebook)
ISBN 9781645277194 (hardcover)
ISBN 9781645277200 (ebook)
Subjects: LCSH: Puma—Juvenile literature.
Classification: LCC QL737.C23 B7244 2021 (print)
LCC QL737.C23 (ebook) | DDC 599.75/24—dc23
LC record available at https://lccn.loc.gov/2020022617
LC ebook record available at https://lccn.loc.gov/2020022618

Editor: Eliza Leahy
Designer: Michelle Sonnek

Photo Credits: Eric Isselee/Shutterstock, cover, 3, 24; Ultrashock/Shutterstock, 1; William Eugene Dummitt/Shutterstock, 4, 23br; through-my-lens/iStock, 5; Francois Gohier/Pantheon/SuperStock, 6–7; Mikhail Kolesnikov/Shutterstock, 8; Dennis Fast/VWPICS/Science Source, 9; Geoffrey Kuchera/Shutterstock, 10–11; Avalon/Getty, 12–13, 23tl; Gary Samples/Getty, 14–15; Michael Durham/Minden Pictures/SuperStock, 16–17; Warren Metcalf/Shutterstock, 18; Dennis W Donohue/Shutterstock, 19, 23tr; Balaraman Arun/Shutterstock, 20–21; LanaG/Shutterstock, 23bl.

Printed in the United States of America at Corporate Graphics in North Mankato, Minnesota.

Table of Contents

Jump and Climb

Whose big tracks are these?

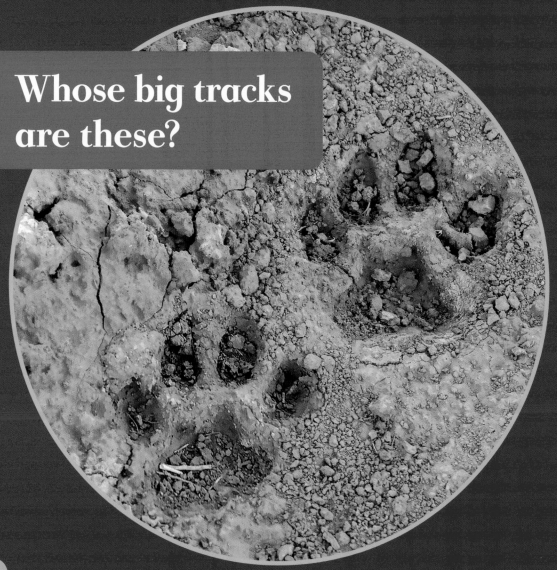

A cougar's!
Cougars are big cats.

5

We also call them mountain lions.

Why?

Many live in the mountains.

claw

Their claws are sharp.

They help cougars climb.

Neat!

These cats have tan fur.
It helps them hide.

11

A cub has spots.

The spots go away.

When?

After a few months.

cub

Cougars jump high.
They jump far, too.

Cougars can see in the dark.
They hunt prey at night.

This one runs
after a deer.

It pounces!

The deer got away.
The cougar sleeps.
It will hunt again
tonight.

Where in the World?

Most cougars live in South America or western North America. Take a look!

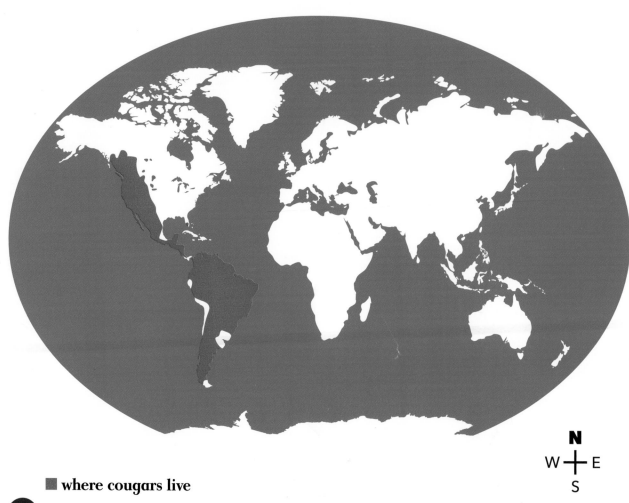

■ where cougars live

Picture Glossary

cub
A young cougar.

pounces
Jumps forward and grabs
something suddenly.

prey
Animals that are hunted
by other animals for food.

tracks
Marks left behind
by a moving animal.

Index

To Learn More

Finding more information is as easy as 1, 2, 3.

❶ Go to www.factsurfer.com

❷ Enter "cougars" into the search box.

❸ Choose your book to see a list of websites.